Praise for *The Secrets of Success*

This is ingenious. "The Secrets of Success" is compact, easy to read and jam packed with valuable information. It's a must read for young and old.

Robert Harris
New York Giants

This is not just an ordinary book of quotations. It is a motivational gem. I couldn't put it down.

Baruti Bediako, C.P.A.
Sankofa Consulting Services

"The Secrets of Success" is thought provoking, refreshing and the artwork is visually attractive.

Edwin Dolores
JEMR Associates

One of these fine days when the African world reaches the pinnacle of liberation and empowerment, we will look back and recognize contributions large and small that helped us break the cycle of dependency and powerlessness. Glenda Taylor's compilation of quotations, "The Secrets of Success," may not hold the rank of general in this army nor will it be a mere buck private; yet, somewhere in between, her work will be counted among the soldierly contributions worthy of mention.

Mamadou Chinyelu
author of Sons of the Prophets

The Secrets of Success

of

Success

Quotations By African-American Achievers

The Secrets of Success

Quotations By African-American Achievers

Glenda R. Taylor

Olympic Vision
PUBLISHERS
New York • 1998

Library of Congress Cataloging - in Publication Data
Taylor, Glenda R., 1955 -

The Secrets of Success / Glenda R. Taylor - 1st ed
p.cm.
ISBN# 0-9662142-0-X
I. Title   1998
1. Success   2. Quotations   98-065370
3. African-Americans   4. Successful African-Americans
5. Reference

Printed in the United States of America.
Cover design & layout by Riley+Velez Design™

First Edition

Olympic Vision Publishers books are available at special quantity discounts when
purchased in bulk by corporations, organizations, or groups. Customized
printings, special arrangements and excerpts can be produced to meet your
needs. For more information, contact Special Markets Manager, Olympic Vision,
475 Riverside Drive, Suite 1940, New York, NY 10115 or call (212) 870-3529.

Dedicated to my ancestors whose journey through the middle passage, the underground railroad, the Jim Crow South and the Civil Rights Movement is an undertold American story which symbolizes the fortitude of the human spirit in the face of brutal adversity; to my mother who told me "there's nothin' you can't do"; and to Oprah the angel among us who allows her divinity to be used to uplift the social and spiritual consciousness of all Americans.

Foreward

As little boys growing up in Bronx, New York, occasionally we got into little fights and scuffles with each other. Our elders would often scold us for doing so and we would plead our case as to who started the altercation and why we reacted with physical force, or threats thereof, by exclaiming, "He called me a name!" And quite frequently the elder would say to us "Sticks and stones may break your bones, but words will never harm you!"

I believe that most of us realize that nothing could be further from the truth. *The word*, written or spoken with knowledge, passion and skill, is one of humankind's most powerful and effective weapons. It is potent whether utilized offensively or defensively and those among us who possess the ability to use words masterfully are potentially powerful people. "The Secrets of Success" contains the potent words of African-Americans who have made a significant contribution to their field.

The power of *the word* is enhanced significantly depending upon how it is communicated. Until the advent of broadcast media, one first had to be able to read, then have access to the limited source of written material, which, until the advent of the printing press, was usually not current information, nor was it widely accessible. Therefore, word of mouth was the primary source of spreading *the word.*

When radio became available, the listener did not have to be literate to participate in the use of the medium. One only needed to have access to a radio. Therefore, if someone wanted to prevent people from getting pertinent information, they had to keep them ignorant and/or deny them access to the word, both of which enhanced the ability of subjugators to control their populace.

Some historical examples of this were the prohibition on teaching slaves to read or write when slavery was the norm in the southern United States; the efforts of a revolutionary or government faction to gain or keep control of the local radio station early in a conflict. Another prime example was the Soviet Union's total control of the communications media throughout our recent history.

The power to control the dissemination of *the word* is akin to the ultimate power in our society. With that power one can influence and shape the attitude and thoughts of the masses. History has shown that most often when this power has been in the hands of a few, the ultimate result was not in the best interest of humankind.

It is irrefutable that the power of positive thinking is an essential element in one's quest to build self-esteem and achieve individual success. To acquire a positive attitude requires receiving *the word* in such a positive and effective manner that it can be perceived as positive even in a negative environment. It is only during the past fifty years that African-Americans have been able to make significant strides towards achieving that status.

During that period, the acquisition of local broadcast and national print media by African-Americans enabled us to begin to disseminate more positive perspectives of ourselves in and outside of our own community. This occurred despite the fact that the circulation and influence of Black newspapers, then the mainstay of "Black-owned media," began to decline. We were able to partially overcome that deficiency because the rapid growth in communications technology enhanced our ability to influence the general media.

Prior to the aforementioned events, the general media basically undermined our self worth, depreciated our character and ignored our heritage. This was not an environment in which we could consistently project a positive *word*.

Today, the world is rapidly becoming engrossed in digital technology. Most notably is the growth of the Internet. Internet technology and the Internet itself represent the greatest opportunity we have ever had to effectively communicate with the world. We must immerse ourselves in every aspect of its development. If we don't, the consequences could be devastating to our future as a people.

The word has no power if it cannot be disseminated. Therefore, it is essential that we have complete accessibility to all types of media as well as a significant degree of control and influence thereof.

"The Secrets of Success" need not be a secret as long as African-Americans have unlimited access to information; and our achievements will continue to be notable if we have the tenacity and determination to put the word to proper use. This book gives us access to the word. The rest is up to you.

Waynett A. Sobers, Jr. is Vice-President of Corporate Communications for Black Enterprise Magazine. *He is also a successful entreprenuer who has sat on the Board of Directors of numerous companies including Earl Graves, Ltd. and Equitable Variable Life Insurance Company.*

Introduction

The biggest secret since reconstruction is that against immeasurable odds African-Americans have risen from slavery and have a substantial net worth. African-Americans have built businesses. They have bought homes. They have gotten an education. They have tasted the apple pie. They have achieved the not so dirty word called success.

Many studies have been done on African-Americans who languish in poverty, pain and despair, unable to free themselves from the shackles, of their past, their environment, their pain. Few studies have been done on the beliefs and ideologies of African-American achievers. How do they think? What made the difference? What keeps them going? Why do they succeed? The words of African-Americans can be a lesson to all Americans. It is a lesson of how to beat the odds.

It is only now in the 90's that the secrets of successful African-Americans are being revealed. It is important that successful African-Americans continue to step from behind the shadows of guilt placed upon them by those who have not succeeded or those who place obstacles before them. They must be heard. Their words must be remembered.

They know the truth. They were no luckier; they just worked harder. They had no more chips; they just didn't give up. Their words must be heard.

Struggle, pain, racism, obstacles. Struggle, dread, fear, hopelessness. Struggle, anguish, discrimination, abuse. Struggle, slavery, despair, heartache.

Determination, rape, violence, lynching. Determination, betrayal, emptiness, apathy. The African-American experience has been all of this. Yet, it has contained some of the greatest, most powerful success stories ever told.

How did they do it? What makes them winners not whiners? Herein, lies the secrets in their own words.

Izell R Glover
-97-

Let the drum beat roll
Let the griots speak
Tell me ...

Glenda R. Taylor

You can't win unless you learn how to lose.

Kareem Abdul-Jabbar

*Y*ou *also need to know history. If you read history, you. . .know that salvation is certain because we have already come through more problems than we face today.*

Na'im Akbar

*Y*ou must know what you want and what you
will settle for...

Humza Al-Hafeez

The Secrets of Success

If there's any secret about my fights, it's how I prepare myself.

Only a man who knows what it is to be defeated can reach down and come up with the extra ounce of power it takes to win when the match is even...He wants the crown, but is he willing to pay the price?...If the price of winning is to be a broken jaw, a smashed nose, a cracked skull, a disfigured face, you pay it if you want to be King...you have to lay it all on the line, back down or be damned forever.

Muhammad Ali

Glenda R. Taylor

*L*ife is pure adventure, and the sooner we realize that, the quicker we will be able to treat life as art: to bring all our energies to each encounter.

Maya Angelou

The Secrets of Success

*A*ll my work is meant to say you may
encounter defeats, but you must not be
defeated. In fact, the encountering may be the
very experience which creates the vitality and the
power to endure.

Maya Angelou

Glenda R. Taylor

*I*n order to win, we pay with energy and effort and discipline.

Maya Angelou

The Secrets of Success

Speak victoriously, dispense with resignation, create excellence, and establish victorious values. Know your history ...

Molefi Kete Asante

The Secrets of Success

*S*truggle *itself becomes an oppression censor
when one cannot see victory.*

Molefi Kete Asante

Glenda R. Taylor

*A*long *the way you will stumble, and perhaps even fall; but that, too, is normal and to be expected. Get up, get back on your feet, chastened, but wiser, and continue down the road.*

Arthur Ashe

Technology is expanding as never before; the instruments of change are everywhere. You will often feel that you don't have enough time to do what you want to do. Make time. Control time; do not let time control you anymore than it must; balance the activity of your life...

Arthur Ashe

Glenda R. Taylor

There is never time in the future in which we will work out our salvation. The challenge is in the moment; the time is always now.

Know whence you come. If you know whence you come, there is really no limit to where you can go.

James Baldwin

The Secrets of Success

*T*he greatest friends any of us have are knowledge and information.

Harry Belafonte

Glenda R. Taylor

Continued struggle can bring about expected benefits and gains that in themselves justify continued endeavor.

Derrick Bell

The Secrets of Success

There is a place in God's sun for the youth farthest down who has the vision, the determination, and the courage to reach it.

Mary McLeod Bethune

Glenda R. Taylor

Nearby was a field. . .which was used as a dumping ground. I approached the owner, determined to buy it. The price was $250.00. In a daze, he finally agreed to take five dollars down, and the balance in two years. I promised to be back in a few days with the initial payment. He never knew it, but I didn't have five dollars. I raised this sum selling ice cream and sweet potato pies to the workmen on the construction jobs, and I took the owner his money in small change wrapped in my handkerchief.

Mary McLeod Bethune

I *have realized that all things I do have to be done to glorify God.*

Todd Bridges

The Secrets of Success

We have already done so much that people call impossible. However, if the bumblebee knew the theory of aerodynamics, he would not be able to fly. But the bumblebee being unaware of scientific truths, goes ahead and flies anyway. If it is possible, we will do it.

Tom Bradley

Glenda R. Taylor

There comes a time when you have to drop your burdens in order to fight for yourself and your dreams.

Our spirits were rich, and we drew strength from the challenge of seeing our visions through to reality.

Les Brown

The Secrets of Success

We microwave our meals, speed-dial our telephones, and zap the channels on our television sets. We've become accustomed to instantaneous results. In spite of what they show you on television ...You must have patience and engage in persistent action toward making your dream become a reality.

Les Brown

The first key is education.

Ron Brown

The Secrets of Success

*T*o succeed as a people, Blacks have to invest in and build their community.

Tony Brown

The Secrets of Success

*I*n this age...the march of progress requires that
we help ourselves. . .If we expect our race to
progress, we must educate our young men and
women.

Charles W. Chestnut

Glenda R. Taylor

*O*ur *Creator is not so unkind to give us a vision without giving us everything else we need to bring the vision to fruition.*

Mamadou Chinyelu

The Secrets of Success

Women should enter the battle of politics and fight it out toe-to-toe with their male counterparts.

Shirley Chisolm

Glenda R. Taylor

I *understood my father's mandate: to strive, to*
excel, to take full advantage of every
educational opportunity offered to me...

Johnny Cochran

The Secrets of Success

A woman without knowledge of who she is cannot successfully participate in determining the direction in which she wishes to go. We need the kind of education that genuinely incorporates the diversity and complexity in women's lives.

Johnetta B. Cole

Thinkers succeed.

Marva Collins

The Secrets of Success

D^{on't} *be afraid to open your eyes and dream.*

Sean "Puffy" Combs

Glenda R. Taylor

*T*he past is a ghost, the future a dream, and all we ever have is now.

Bill Cosby

If you want to be the best...you've got to work harder than anybody else.

Sammy Davis, Jr.

The Secrets of Success

Change, destroy and rebuild...Seize the time.

Angela Davis

Glenda R. Taylor

I just laugh it off. I never let prejudice stop me from what I wanted to do in this life.

Sadie Delany

The Secrets of Success

*A*s you live, believe in life! Always human
beings will live and progress to a greater
broader and fuller life.

W. E. B. DuBois

Glenda R. Taylor

The Secrets of Success

From my earliest recollection, I date the entertainment of a deep conviction that slavery would not always be able to hold me within its foul embrace; and in the darkest hours of my career in slavery, this living word of faith and spirit of hope departed not from me, but remained like ministering angels to cheer me through the gloom.

Frederick Douglass

Glenda R. Taylor

There's no free lunch.

Marian Wright Edelman

*I*f you want to get out of the fields, get something in your head.

*D*o your best; that's not good enough.

Joycelyn Elders, M.D.

Glenda R. Taylor

*T*o *be successful and reach your goal you must first remove the barriers in your mind. These are the obstacles to your success. A "yes I can" attitude will overcome barriers and when the way is clear, your goal will be in sight.*

Reginald English

*T*he ballot is one of the keys to the solution...

*W*e're going to get Negroes registered and voting...with that basic political power we'll continue working toward economic strength.

Medgar Evers

Glenda R. Taylor

We ought to be a little more wise with the money we have.

Louis Farrakhan

Everybody wants to be somebody. The thing you have to do is give them confidence. You have to give a kid a dream.

George Foreman

Glenda R. Taylor

*A*ny *kind of happiness starts with a good home life. People can be rich, or they can be a political success, but unless they have a good home life...they don't have anything at all...*

Aretha Franklin

The Secrets of Success

We believe that by working together for the good of all of our people, we all will benefit and, more important, our children and the world they grow in will benefit.

George C. Fraser

The Secrets of Success

No matter how low they fall, they can get back up; no matter how many times they stumble, they can still walk tall. That neither racism nor sexism can stop a determined mind, or a heart beating with love for the very body that carries it. It is a lesson for all people, regardless of race or sex; for anyone who has had to rise to a challenge.

Patrice Gaines

Glenda R. Taylor

You can't expect anything to come easy.

Cheryl Gamble

The Secrets of Success

Lift up yourselves, men, take yourselves out of the myrrh and hitch your hopes to the stars; yes rise as high as the very stars themselves. Let no man pull you down...

Marcus Garvey

Glenda R. Taylor

The Secrets of Success

*U*p! *Up! You mighty race. You can accomplish what you will.*

Marcus Garvey

*P*eople *become what they think they are.*

*J*ust *because I wasn't doing well in school didn't mean I had to be dumb. . .intelligence and education were two different things. If you had both of them you had it made. But if you could only have one. . .it'd better be intelligence.*

Berry Gordy, Jr.

*P*lan more and work less.

*T*he power of somebody believing in you, or convincing you that they believe in you works wonders.

Berry Gordy, Jr.

Build wealth first by looking within. Start a business. Invest in the black community with your time and money. Patronize other black-owned businesses. Hire black people to work for you. Form alliances and partnerships with other black businesspeople. Network with each other for your mutual benefit. Reduce your debt. Increase your savings. Put money into assets that have long-term value....

Earl G. Graves

Never turn away someone who can be of assistance to you purely because of race. Your mission is far too important for that.

Earl G. Graves

Glenda R. Taylor

Nothing is more powerful and liberating than knowledge.

William H. Gray, III

The Secrets of Success

You didn't die a slave for nothing, momma. You brought us up. You and all those Negro mothers who gave their kids strength to go on, to take a thimble to the well while the whites were taking buckets. Those of us who weren't destroyed got stronger, got calluses on our souls...

Dick Gregory

Glenda R. Taylor

*E*ach of us becomes more powerful when we work together.

(Carol) Lani Guinier

The secret is keeping busy, and loving what you do.

I pray and practice a lot.

Lionel Hampton

Glenda R. Taylor

When you're a black woman, you seldom get to do what you just want to do; you always do what you have to do.

Dorothy Height

If I don't have friends, then I ain't got nothing.

Billie Holliday

The Secrets of Success

There is a quality to life in which risks are taken that a safe life can never duplicate.

Ellen Holly

Glenda R. Taylor

We make our future by the best use of the present.

Zora Neale Hurston

*Y*our experience of prosperity begins with your decision to prosper.

*U*se the technique of visualization. You must see the goals you have set for yourself.

Reverend Ike

Glenda R. Taylor

*D*efine *what you want to be, what you want to do, and what you want to have.*

Reverend Ike

The Secrets of Success

I surround myself with messages like the 77th Psalm, because I know how powerful words are. . .I fill my environment with positive words and images to keep me on track.

LL Cool J

The Secrets of Success

If you want to make the world a better place, take a look at yourself and make a change. Start with the man in the mirror.

Michael Jackson

Glenda R. Taylor

When Black people, corporations and institutions who have achieved success can share it with those who are still involved in the struggle for it, we are moving in the right direction.

Jesse Jackson

The Secrets of Success

I've learned to live with rage. In some ways, its my rage that keeps me going. Without it, I would have been whipped long ago. With it, I got a lot more songs to sing.

Etta James

Glenda R. Taylor

You have to understand and believe in yourself and do what it is you know you are capable of in spite of what anyone else may tell you.

Mae Jemison

The Secrets of Success

I *do believe that being on the planet is an opportunity we're given - a chance to work and improve to become the best we possibly can be.*

Beverly Johnson

Glenda R. Taylor

*T*he only way that we as Black people are going to get anything is through ownership, because ownership brings power.

*S*tick with what you do best.

Earvin "Magic" Johnson

To succeed one must be creative and persistent.

John H. Johnson

Glenda R. Taylor

What the Black man must do now is look down at the ground upon which he stands, and claim it as his own.

Leroi Jones (Imamu Amiri Baraka)

The Secrets of Success

You've got to keep doing it. . .You'd better be burning every time. If you're not burning, somebody's going to be right behind you burning.

Quincy Jones

Glenda R. Taylor

If you worry too much about what people think or what problems they may have with who you are, you may get bogged down with things that don't really matter.

Gaynelle Griffin Jones

The Secrets of Success

*D*on't prepare for failure. Lose with a defiance.
Write down what went wrong. Get back to it.
*Recognize for the future what it is... Failure is a
wholly necessary part of the process, the stuff of
heroes and legends.*

Michael Jordan

The Secrets of Success

If you run into a wall, don't turn around and give up. Figure out how to climb it, go through it, or work around it.

Michael Jordan

Glenda R. Taylor

*F**ailure always makes me try harder.*

Michael Jordan

The Secrets of Success

*L*ong distance running, which requires planning, pacing, discipline and stamina, and a belief in the ability to win over everything over the long haul...Lasting power is the name of the game.

John Killens

*T*he key to networking success is to nurture your network so that you can tap into the talents and skills and knowledge of hundreds of people.

*R*ise above any petty differences and focus on the power of interdependence.

Dennis Kimbro

The Secrets of Success

*L*et no fire consume your hopes for a brighter *tomorrow...Let no fear dominate you or hold you back. If you want to achieve excellence, it's up to you.*

Bernice King

Glenda R. Taylor

If you are able to experience adversity and rise above it, then that in itself builds character.

Dexter King

The Secrets of Success

I learned to confront head on things that had been troubling me, and to go after those that I had been searching for. . . Most important, I learned to take responsibility for my own happiness.

Gladys Knight

Glenda R. Taylor

*W*e must not let the fact that we are victims of injustice lull us into abrogating responsibility for our own lives.

*H*e may be uneducated or poverty stricken, but these handicaps must not prevent him from seeing that he has within his being the power to alter his fate.

Martin Luther King, Jr.

Glenda R. Taylor

Once I stopped dwelling on what I didn't have, on what I thought I was going to lose, and began to give freely, everything opened up for me. I have learned to face the worst tragedy with the best attitude - with grace and style and courage.

Patti LaBelle

The Secrets of Success

Cut your losses and keep your chin up regardless of what happens.

Reginald Lewis

Glenda R. Taylor

*P*rogress is healing the wound.

Malcolm X

The Secrets of Success

It's the work you do inside yourself that makes you on the outside a man.

Terry McMillan

Glenda R. Taylor

Whether or not you reach your goals in life depends entirely on how well you prepare for them and how badly you want them...

Ronald McNair

The Secrets of Success

If they try and believe in themselves, and if they believe in God—especially in America—anything is possible.

Kenya Moore

Glenda R. Taylor

*T*he secret of success is persistence, *perserverance and risk taking and all of that has to be cushioned by faith.*

Celeste Morris

The Secrets of Success

You win by preparation and experience, that's all.

Constance Baker Motley

The Secrets of Success

My father always said there are only two things that you have to do in life. You have to pay rent and you have to do what you love.

Walter Mosley

Glenda R. Taylor

*A*s long as people recognize the beauty of their human spirits and work against suppression and exploitation, they will be carrying out the most beautiful ideas of all time.

Huey P. Newton

The Secrets of Success

To humble yourself does not mean you are weak...It's a sign of strength...in your heart you know your inner strength, you know who you are, and that's all that matters...

Hakeem Olajuwon

Glenda R. Taylor

I *used to sit and dream in huge silence.*

I *dreamt big.*

Gordon Parks, Sr.

The Secrets of Success

There is nothing more noble than a good try.

Gordon Parks, Sr.

The Secrets of Success

*S uccess is filled with the agony of how and why
. . .it takes you down a lonely road and you
feel, at times that you are traveling it alone. You
can only keep walking. During the loneliness you
get to know who you are. Then you face the
choice - of keeping everybody's friendship, or
losing the one you have made with yourself. . .*

Gordon Parks, Sr.

Glenda R. Taylor

I have learned throughout my life that what really matters is not whether we have problems but how we go through whatever we are facing.

Rosa Parks

The Secrets of Success

No matter what the circumstances are, it is best to pursue behavior that is above reproach, because then you will be respected for your actions.

Rosa Parks

Glenda R. Taylor

Sometimes one must make painful choices, but we must think of others as well.

Perhaps my only 'secret' is my attitude toward life.

It is important to keep yourself grounded in faith. When things are not going the way you want, you must keep hope alive...

Rosa Parks

The Secrets of Success

Strong families raise strong, healthy children.

Alvin F. Poussaint, M.D.

113

The Secrets of Success

You just realize that survival is day to day and you start to grasp your own spirit, you start to grasp the depth of the human spirit, and you start to understand your own ability to cope no matter what.

Melba Pattillo

Glenda R. Taylor

We must turn our energies inwardly toward our homes, our churches, our families, our children, our colleges, our neighborhoods, our businesses, and our communities. . .There is no time for cotillions and tears.

Adam Clayton Powell, Jr.

The Secrets of Success

There are no secrets to success. . .Success is the result of perfection, hard work, learning from failure, loyalty to those for whom you work, and persistence. . .

Colin Powell

I always remember to keep sunshine on my face.

Richard Pryor

I *realize that although I can't undo what's already happened, I can learn from it.*

Robin Quivers

Glenda R. Taylor

Find something you like to do so much you would do it even if you weren't paid for it, something that the joy of it is all that makes you love to do it. And it will make you wealthy.

Della Reese

119

The Secrets of Success

Don't worry about the doors, keep your eyes open for the windows of life that lead you to the new horizons the Lord has planned for you ...

Della Reese

Glenda R. Taylor

The grass may look greener on the other side, but its just as hard to cut.

*M*ass action — in political life and elsewhere is
Negro power in motion; and it is the way to
win.

Paul Robeson

Glenda R. Taylor

*T*he challenges of events call for clarity of vision and unity of action.

Paul Robeson

The Secrets of Success

I needed to leave all that street crap in my past and move on with my life. I put my mind forward and decided to make it, and I left a lot behind...But I didn't forget my roots...I go back there for perspective because sometimes I need it. It keeps me grounded.

Dennis Rodman

The Secrets of Success

C *losing one door, another one opens.*

Diana Ross

Glenda R. Taylor

All our dreams can come true if we have the courage to believe. The dreamer and the dream become one.

I don't have all the answers, but at least I know I'll take my share of chances.

Diana Ross

I *found out in life that you always have a choice. Some of the choices you may not particularly like, but you have a choice.*

Richard Roundtree

Glenda R. Taylor

It's always easy to blame...I take responsibility for my actions.

Richard Roundtree

The Secrets of Success

We must all start seeing ourselves beginning to seize the time.

Bobby Seale

Glenda R. Taylor

Choose the good and praise it.

Betty Shabazz

*C**hoose heroes, the right heroes. Choose people who have the posture and qualities that you want to have and don't be afraid to evaluate them. And those of you coming out of single parent homes, look for alternative role models and be very careful whom you choose.*

Al Sharpton

The Secrets of Success

*H*ave *Dreams. . .and remember dreams are democratic, you can dream in a jail cell, in a hospital bed, in a shack or shanty, in the projects or in a mansion.*

Al Sharpton

Glenda R. Taylor

Whoever you are, learn your roots, find out your roots, find out who your people are, where they came from, what it took them to arrive at the place you find yourself. Whether that place be a housing project or Scarsdale, the only way you are going to progress is to build on what came before...

Al Sharpton

135

The Secrets of Success

You can never have too many prayers going.

O.J. Simpson

Glenda R. Taylor

The reason I am what I am today is because I had a mother and father who cared enough to keep me in line, but who also always allowed me to dream my dreams.

Sinbad

The Secrets of Success

*Y*ou should cultivate your mind, spirit, body, heart and soul.

Sistah Souljah

Glenda R. Taylor

Youngsters need to think more broadly in terms of career options. There is more out there than just high-profile, high income professions.

Lisa Stevens

The Secrets of Success

There is no such thing as "can't." See your goals in your mind's eye. Know that you can achieve them. Work tirelessly, garnering, developing and utilizing resources... and success will be yours.

Mary J. Taylor

Glenda R. Taylor

We are at our best when we are surrounded by happy, healthy people, people who hold a positive vision...people who tell us the truth.

Staying centered each moment puts you in charge of your life.

Susan Taylor

*Y*our mind is a profile author; what you believe composes your life.

*W*e have to choose our friends wisely and never abandon common sense.

Susan Taylor

Glenda R. Taylor

*B*rain *power will liberate you.*

C. Delores Tucker

The Secrets of Success

Buddhism changed my old patterns of thought — it taught me how to be a positive thinker. It helps you to stop saying 'What I can't do and what I can't have, and start saying, what I am going to do.' I never allowed myself to get lost even when I was a little girl. I held on to the positive side. I never gave in to alcohol, never gave in to drugs, not even smoking. I gave in to myself. I went inside of me to help me.

Tina Turner

Glenda R. Taylor

I was in an institution. . .and Muhammad Ali came there one day, and I said, that's what I want to be, I want to be the champ of the world.

Mike Tyson

*A*greements give clarity. They bring about order and understanding. Agreements are an important element to success.

Iyanla Vanzant

The Secrets of Success

The universe responds. What you ask of it, it gives.

Alice Walker

Glenda R. Taylor

No person is your friend who demands your silence; or denies your right to grow.

Alice Walker

The Secrets of Success

*W*ring *success out of a number of business opportunities that knock at your door. . . don't sit down and wait for opportunities to come...get up and make them.*

Madam C.J. Walker

The Secrets of Success

There will be setbacks. There will be people who try and put a noose around you and put stumbling blocks [before you]. You just keep going at it.

Leroy T. Walker

Glenda R. Taylor

The individual who can do something that the world wants, done well, in the end, makes his way regardless of race.

I have learned that success is to be measured not so much by the position one has reached in life as by the obstacles which he has overcome while trying to succeed.

Booker T. Washington

The Secrets of Success

We can affect more people positively than people can affect us negatively.

Denzel Washington

The key to my success other than the greater good is my family.

Denzel Washington

The Secrets of Success

*Y*ou *have to take control of your destiny and
if your destiny is full of negativity then that
first thing you have to do is sweep up your house.*

Rolonda Watts

None of us alone can save the nation or world. But each of us can make a positive difference if we commit ourselves to do so.

Cornell West

The Secrets of Success

*L**earning from others is one of the best tools for*
success.

Terrie Williams

Glenda R. Taylor

*M**arketing yourself is one of the most important ways to get ahead in this world.*

Terrie Williams

The Secrets of Success

*B*e twice as ambitious, twice as motivated and
have twice the goals.

Demond Wilson

*F*or everyone of us that succeeds, it's because
there's somebody there to show you the way
out.

*Y*ou get a chance every day to redefine who
you are.

*T*here is nothing greater than the spirit within
you.

Oprah Winfrey

The Secrets of Success

*T*here are so many pieces to the process that have helped me be who I am. It's something as small as seeing Diana Ross and the Supremes. I remember the night I was ten years old and Sidney Poitier received the Academy Award...And I thought to myself, I'm going to be there.

Oprah Winfrey

Glenda R. Taylor

*G*oing back to that beautiful history. . .it is *going to inspire us to greater achievements.*

Carter G. Woodson

The Secrets of Success

Editor's Note

When I was barely 19 years old, I was beaming with joy and enthusiasm. I felt life had endless possibilities. I went on a never ending path which introduced me to hundreds of philosophers, poets, metaphysicians, spiritual leaders, motivational speakers; what I refer to as success technicians. Their words had a tremendous impact on me because they reiterated what my mother had always told me - "there's nothin' that you can't do." But, I was at a crossroads. Only a few years had passed, since I had first been introduced to Julius Lester's book "To Be A Slave" and learned about a place called South Africa and a man named Nelson Mandela who opposed apartheid. I was at a crossroads and I was being seduced by the anger of pain.

1977. I had just truly understood the history of the African-American in America and the people of the diaspora. I was a New Yorker, so even though I was born in the midst of the burgeoning civil rights movement, I was only now learning about Jim Crow and Rosa Parks. Growing up, I experienced New York racism which is much different though no less damaging than southern racism. But my mother born and raised in the south, fled to New York and somehow to her credit shielded me and my sister from the jaws of defeat, dread and despair that being beaten by the whips of hatred and inhumanity creates.

My mother told us that everyone was the same and that we should hate no one. We grew up with Christian white people who were friendly and did not openly show their prejudices, especially not to two cute little Black girls. We grew up in a religion that preached that everyone was equal and that we were one race, the human race. Maybe it was the times. Maybe it was her unique style, but being told all my life that "there's nothing that you can't do" somehow created a child who was allowed to dream of infinite possibilities.

But, I was at a crossroads. After reading the history of my people in America, after understanding my roots, after dancing to Manu Dibango's "Soul Makossa" and Olatunji's "Drums of Passion," after listening to the words of Nikki Giovanni and Dick Gregory, after tangoing with Robert DeCoy's "Nigger Bible", after going to

166

West Africa and being taken into another realm, I was not confused, but shaken. What walk should I walk? What talk should I talk?

Should I hate or should I love? Should I trust or could I trust? If I trust, who should I trust? Trust?

1974. With beautiful skies, winds blowing eagerly, majestically and smoldering, volcanic ash in the air, erupting faster than anyone could sensibly assess, our nation was being rocked at its core - our president, the president of the United States of America embattled in scandal - Watergate- resigns.

What is this? What is happening? In my lifetime, a president resigns; a president, the most powerful man in America, is murdered; a president's brother is killed; men who exert their right to free speech such as Malcolm X and men who teach love your enemy such as Martin Luther King, gunned down, executed. In my lifetime, my short lifetime.

There are many directions that we can take in life. Life is full of choices. One's personal, cultural, family, societal and spiritual history, all has an impact on these choices. The choices I made were not as important as why I made those choices.

I made my choices because I was influenced by the voices, the words, the beliefs, the philosophies of great men and women who touched something deep within my being. The voices started with my mother's constant verbiage challenging any detours in a direction unsuitable for a child worthy of the best life had to offer.

My journey outward, at 19 years old, beyond the comforting sounds of the womb began with my belief that all things were possible, regardless of race, color, creed or disability. But, once my young mind understood the racial atrocities committed against people of African descent, a natural conflict in this belief system was created. Institutional racism stood like a glass wall between me and the success to which I knew I was entitled.

Then, of course, there was sexism. I was female and mother never told me that I had a place beneath my dreams because I was female. Yet, "reality" showed that women had a place in society. There was a line which they could not cross. Wow! a double whammy: African-American and female. How could the Judeo-Christian belief that all things are possible be true?

I made a decision. I held on to my belief that all things were possible. I felt that it must include me, even though I was a member of a race of people who were fighting oppression for the last three hundred years. And I knew being female didn't thwart my mother's dreams, so I decided that if I were going to succeed, the best thing for me to do was to find out what successful people had in common and follow their system.

I was at a crossroads and people I never met, but felt I knew fed me. I eagerly read Robert Schuller, Napoleon Hill and W. Clement Stone. I learned that Napoleon Hill had done the same thing I was doing. He studied successful people and found out their secrets. "Think and Grow Rich" and "The Success System That Never Fails" were invaluable.

The words in these books were like apple seeds, nurturing dreams through the sheer use of simple language. I drank every word, especially the success stories of African-Americans and women like Madam C.J. Walker. These stories were scarce in the early seventies, but I didn't care. Each story was further proof to me that my goals were attainable.

I was at a crossroads. I always read a lot, undeviating, in my quest through the inexhaustible shrines of thought — called books — beckoning me into worlds I had not known. I flew and ran and walked through these worlds, learning secrets, exploring ideas, untangling the enigma which had me searching for a way to fulfill a yearning residing deep within my being, a yearning I knew not from whence it came.

Ultimately, I learned the secrets of success. I used them and continue to use them. When I do the human thing of not doing what I know works, I simply do not accomplish what I know that I could. I learned that we can be influenced by those we know and those we do not know. I learned that words are very powerful and that we have a responsibility to use our words carefully.

I, also, learned to love. I learned to love myself and my people.

I learned to love my country for all its strengths and weaknesses. And I learned that the journey of African-American people, once learned, appreciated and understood, truly symbolizes an ongoing quest and realization of the American dream.

I learned that success is possible and the American Dream can be realized, be you Black or white or young or old or physically fit or physically challenged. I learned that as Americans we have an ongoing responsibility to make America work. Our constitution and the Declaration of Independence is based on great ideals. These ideals did not always mean all of the people, all of the time, but it is our responsibility and charge as citizens whose blood, sweat and pain help lay the foundation of this country to insure that our government is always working towards the ideals of our country's forefathers.

I learned that success is a process and that we all have a responsibility to each other, our families, our communities, and our country; our greatest responsibility being to our young people and future generations.

I felt obliged to share this knowledge with others, most specifically, young people and this compulsion led to the development of an organization which I founded, Olympic Vision. The mission of Olympic Vision is to teach young people (and their families) that they have the power within to create realities beyond the prisons of their environment. This book propels that mission by exploring the secrets of successful African-Americans.

The most disturbing thing that I realized early on my path is that America's young people are not being taught how to succeed in a systematic way. African-American young people, specifically those in overcrowded urban areas with parents who are burdened by severe socio-economic conditions, are learning a distorted definition of the word success. Why? Because they nor their families nor their teachers nor their peers believe that success is possible.

An even more disturbing trend is that the young people of today have not learned how to dream. Overburdened by the gruesome and shocking realities which confront them, losing their innocence before they are adolescents, America's young people are giving up on their futures.

At a time that many of the world's young still look to America for its ideas, its fashion, its music, its culture, American youth are killing each other, their future, America's future, seemingly, without cause.

If we truly are concerned with the future of our nation, if we are truly concerned with welfare reform, gangs, violence, drugs and teenage pregnancy, if we truly want to save America from drowning in the mire of self-destruction, we can no longer just study the cause of dread and despair. We must act.

We must start by looking back at our rich history and using it as a source of strength not a reason for weakness. We must listen, study and learn from successful African-Americans. They have succeeded against all odds and it is important that we impart this knowledge to our young. We must make them understand that success is possible and we must teach them how to prosper.

How is this process started? What is the first step? The first step is planting the ideas, the thoughts, the beliefs of those who have overcome innumerable obstacles to succeed into the minds and hearts of our young.

This is not merely a book of quotations. This is a book of ideas, philosophies, methods, and beliefs which have propelled these African-Americans to success. It is a book for the young, the old, the successful and the disenfranchised. It is a book that can uplift and motivate.

For those who are seeking success, do not just read this book and put it on a shelf. Memorize these words. Use them as affirmations. Absorb these thoughts. Live these ideas. Make them yours. For these are the secrets of success.

Glenda R. Taylor
October 16, 1997
New York

Biographical Notes

Abdul-Jabbar, Kareem (1947 -   ) Professional basketball player
Akbar, Na'im (1944 -   ) Psychologist, author, educator
Al-Hafeez, Humza (1930 -   ) Entrepreneur, minister
Ali, Muhammad (1942 -   ) Professional boxer, philanthropist
Angelou, Maya (1928 -   ) Author, poet, playwright
Asante, Molefi Kete (1942 -   ) Educator
Ashe, Arthur (1943 - 1993) Tennis professional
Atkins, David (Sinbad) (1956 -   ) Comedian, actor
Baldwin, James (1924 - 1987) Writer
Baraka, Imamu Amiri (Leroi Jones) (1934 -   ) Poet, playwright
Belafonte, Harry (1927 -   ) Singer, actor, civil rights activist
Bell, Derrick (1930 -   ) Educator, author, constitutional law scholar
Bethune , Mary McLeod (1875 - 1955) Educator, Bethune Cookman College founder
Bradley, Tom (1917 - 1998) Former Mayor of Los Angeles
Bridges, Todd (1964 -   ) Actor
Brown, Les (-   ) Motivational speaker, author
Brown, Ronald A. (1941 - 1997) First African-American U.S. Secretary of Commerce
Brown, Tony (1933 -   ) Commentator, writer, producer
Chestnut, Charles (1858 - 1932) Novelist
Chinyelu, Mamadou (1951 -   ) Novelist, folklorist, entrepreneur
Chisolm, Shirley (1924 -   ) Politician
Cochran, Johnny (1937 -   ) Attorney
Cole, Johnetta B. (1936 -   ) Educational administrator, scholar
Collins, Marva (1936 -   ) Educator
Combs, Sean "Puffy" (1970 -   ) Business executive, singer
Cosby, William H. (Bill) (1937 -   ) Actor, comedian
Davis, Angela (1944 -   ) Political activist, educator, author
Davis, Sammy, Jr. (1926 - 1990) Entertainer
Delany, Sadie (1889 -   ) Educator, author
Douglass, Frederick (c. 1817 - 1895) Orator, abolitionist
DuBois, W.E.B. (1868 - 1963) Educator, author, Pan-Africanist
Eikerenkietter, Frederick J., II (Reverend Ike) (1935 -   ) Minister
Edelman, Marian W. (1939 -   ) Children's Defense Fund founder and President
Elders, Jocelyn (1933 -   ) Educator, first African-American U.S. Surgeon General
English, Reginald (1948 -   ) Business executive
Evers, Medgar (1925 - 1963) Civil Rights activist
Farrakhan, Louis (1933 -   ) Clergyman, leader of the Nation of Islam
Foreman, George (1949 -   ) Professional boxer, minister
Franklin, Aretha (1942 -   ) Singer, entertainer
Fraser, George C. (1945 -   ) Business executive
Gaines, Patrice (-   ) Writer
Gamble, Cheryl (-   )

Garvey, Marcus (1887 - 1940) Pan-African theorist
Gordy, Berry, Jr. (1929 -) Business executive, producer, composer
Graves, Earl G. (1935 -) Publisher, media executive
Gray, William H., III (1941 -) President United Negro College Fund
Gregory, Dick (1932 -) Civil rights activist, comedian, author
Guinier, Carol Lani (-) Attorney, educator
Hampton, Lionel (1908 -) Musician
Height, Dorothy (1912 -) Association executive
Holliday, Billie (1915 - 1959) Singer
Holly, Ellen (1931 -) Actress
Hurston, Zora Neale (1903 - 1960) Writer
Ike, Reverend, (See Eikerenkietter, Frederick J., II)
Jackson, Jesse L. (1941 -) Minister, civil rights activist, author
Jackson, Michael (1958 -) Singer, composer, poet, philanthropist, King of Pop
James, Etta (1938 -) Singer
Jemison, Mae (1956 -) Astronaut, physician
Johnson, Beverly (1952 -) Model, actress, singer
Johnson, Earvin, Jr. "Magic" (1959 -) Basketball player, business executive
Johnson, John H. (1918 -) Publishing company executive
Jones, Gaynelle Griffin (-)
Jones, Leroi (See Baraka, Imamu Amiri)
Jones, Quincy (1933 -) Trumpeter, arranger, producer
Jordan, Michael (1963 -) Professional basketball player
Killens, John (1916 - 1987) Writer, civil rights activist
Kimbro, Dennis (1950 -) Educator, author
King, Bernice (1963 -) Cleric, attorney
King, Dexter (1961 -) Business Executive
King, Martin Luther, Jr. (1929 - 1968) Civil and human rights activist, minister, author
Knight, Gladys (1944-) Singer
Labelle, Patti (1944-) Singer, actress, author
Lewis, Reginald (1942- 1993) Business executive
L.L. Cool J. (1968-) Singer, actor
Malcolm X (1925-1965) Black Nationalist, minister
Mcmillan, Terry L. (1951-) Novelist, educator
McNair, Ronald (1950-1986) Astronaut
Moore, Kenya (-) Miss U.S.A.1993, model
Morris, Celeste (1949-) Entrepreneur, political strategist, publisher
Mosley, Walter (1952-) Novelist, screenwriter
Motley, Constance Baker (1921-) First African-American female federal judge
Newton, Huey (1942-1989) Political activist
Olajuwan, Hakeem (1963-) Professional basketball player
Parks, Gordon, Sr. (1912-) Photographer, writer, director, composer
Parks, Rosa (1914-) Civil rights activist

Pattillo, Melba (1943 -) One of the Little Rock Nine students, recipient NAACP Spingarn Medal

Pouissant, Alvin F. (1934 -) Educator, psychiatrist

Powell, Adam Clayton, Jr. (1908 - 1972) Former U.S. Representative

Powell, Colin L. (1937 -) First African-American Chairman of the Joint Chiefs of Staff

Pryor, Richard (1940 -) Comedian, actor

Quivers, Robin (1952 -) Radio talk show host

Reese, Della (1932 -) Singer, actress

Richard, Little (1932 -) Singer, pianist, King of Rock and Roll

Robeson, Paul (1898 - 1976) Actor, singer, civil rights activist

Rodman, Dennis (1961 -) Professional basketball player

Ross, Diana (1944 -) Singer

Roundtree, Richard (1942 -) Actor

Seale, Bobby (1936 -) Black Panther Party co-founder

Shabazz, Betty (1936 - 1997) Civil rights activist

Sharpton, Al (1954 -) Social activist, cleric

Simpson, O.J. (1947 -) Football player, actor

Sinbad (see Atkins, David)

Souljah, Sistah (1964 -) Activist, author

Stevens, Lisa (-) Music industry executive

Taylor, Mary (1937 -) Educational administrator, writer

Taylor, Susan (1946 -) Magazine editor, author

Tucker, Delores C. (1927 -) Newspaper executive

Turner, Tina (1941 -) Singer, entertainer

Tyson, Mike (1966 -) Professional boxer

Vanzant, Iyanla (1953 -) Author, motivational speaker

Walker, Alice (1944 -) Poet, novelist

Walker, Leroy (1918 -) Educator, coach

Walker, Madam C. J. (1867 - 1919) Entrepreneur

Washington, Booker T. (1856 - 1915) Political activist, educator

Washington, Denzel (1954 -) Actor

Watts, Rolanda (1959 -) Talk show host

West, Cornell (1953 -) Educator, educational administrator, author

Williams, Terrie M. (1954 -) Public relations executive

Wilson, Demond (1946 -) Actor, evangelist

Winfrey, Oprah (1954 -) Talk show host, actress, producer, entrepreneur

Woodson, Carter G. (1875 - 1950) Scholar, historian

Index

Acknowledgements

To Yogi Gupta for lifting my spirit; Robert Schuller for teaching me about apple seeds; Mom, Shay, and all my family of friends: Janice Berthoud, Pelham Bollers, Frances Greer, Vivian Holliday, Elizabeth Nunez, Mary Richardson, Babatunde Salau, Margaree Stewart and Karen Teshira - for their on-going support and encouragement; Oswald Bunbury, Sr. for being Ossie; Jade Banks for using the secrets to overcome her obstacles; Jesse Velez for his creativity and sense of humor; Mamadou Chinyelu for lessons about the publishing industry; and Wannaporn Wannachaiwong, Deryck Kingston, Kalia Smith and Karen Bryant for typing services.

About the Editor

Glenda R. Taylor was born in Brooklyn, New York and lived there until December 1989 when she moved to Manorville, New York. Best known for her pioneering work with non-profit human service providers, Taylor has authored over one hundred proposals which have resulted in funding of over $45.5 million. Her mission in life is to share the secrets of success with the millions of Americans who she says, "are thirsty, before a fountain of water."

Taylor is Chief Executive Officer and founder of Olympic Vision, a non-profit organization, developed to foster the growth of young people so that they can use their creative energies to cure the economic, social and environmental ills of our society.

Called a visionary by the *New York Daily Challenge*, Taylor is listed in the International Biographical Centre's *"The World's Who's Who of Women,"* The Biographical Institute's *"Two Thousand Notable Women,"* and has received a Certificate for Outstanding Service to Youth from the New York State Division for Youth.

About the Artists

Izell Glover is an internationally known artist, best known for his series on the Black West. Glover is currently working on a book of his work which spans the past thirty-five years.

Lauchland Pelle is known for his illustrations in comic books. He has done pencil art for D.C. Comics, Brain Storm Comics and Dark Horse Publications and illustrations for FPJ Graphics and the Larkin group.